WASTE NOT, WANT NOT

WHY WE WILL NEVER WIN ANOTHER WAR!!

J.T. STORM

authorHOUSE®

AuthorHouse™
1663 Liberty Drive, Suite 200
Bloomington, IN 47403
www.authorhouse.com
Phone: 1-800-839-8640

First published by AuthorHouse 5/12/2009

ISBN: 978-1-4389-4853-9 (sc)

Library of Congress Control Number: 2009901975

Printed in the United States of America
Bloomington, Indiana

This book is printed on acid-free paper.

FOREWORD

First I want to thank everyone that has read my first book and that I hoped you at the very least learned something, either about the "WAR" on Terror or about yourself? If so then I think it was sure worth your time to read it, don't you? Now whether you liked it or you didn't like it you can at least say that it was interesting. That is all that I was after, to give a truthful representation as to what goes on a daily basis in a combat zone. Everything is not pretty and everything is not going to be your cup of tea, but at least you have a better understanding of what goes on with the brave men and women who we have fighting for us throughout the world.

Some people have told me that it sounded like I was real angry and that I seem to be ranting about this or that? Well folks I did not write a poetry book or fictional romance story, I wrote about WAR! And that is never going to be pretty, no matter how you try and represent it. Those are just facts, not my impressions, just facts.

At the time the first book was written, I was a part of the "SURGE" which more and more will show in years gone by that it actually made a difference. To know how much of a difference will only be determined in years to come, probably a lot of years from now, but never the less, it will show that a considerable difference was made during this particular period of the War and I am proud and honored that I was able to be a part of and to help in some small way in that part of history.

Now what you are going to read in the following pages may make you angry, sad, laugh or even shake your head in disbelief! But I want to say that I hope you take what is written into context. I hope in some small way that the right person or persons read this book try to take some type of corrective action to better the situation and to make it better. That is the sole purpose of writing this book and having a title with the name it has. I want to get peoples attention and psychology and history have shown that when people get angry or frustrated that they are more likely to change? For better or for worse? We will see, only time will tell. All can do is bring things to light that probably are known by a small fraction of the population, yet most of what is written here is public knowledge and anyone and everyone could look this information up on the internet yourself, and I hope you do.

Only when something is brought to your attention is the problem completely addressed! That is a reactionary approach; I want to give you something to think about so you might take the pro-active approach and strive to be the best each and everyone of can be, in the greatest country in the world.

CHAPTER 1

Vietnam was just the beginning, in the pages to follow you will be given incidents, practices, policies and reasons why the United States will never win another war. At the end you will be able to make your own conclusions, but all I ask is that you be honest with yourself. Now I know everyone will have their own opinion, that's fine. I am certainly not trying to make you change your opinion, we are just going to talk about a few things that probably the average U.S. citizen had no knowledge of. Hey, and for all you military retirees or still active, you cannot tell me shit! Why, because I have been there and done that in the military and also on the private side, so if you are military retired or still active if you do not want to read what you probably know is true, then go ahead and close this book, or throw it away. But if you would like to read why I wrote what I wrote in the first few lines then read on!! You will be amazed, confused, mad, sad and probably laugh somewhere along the way, but hey, that's good, right? Everybody likes to laugh a little, I know I do!! But being around was and involved with war sometimes can give you some weird distorted sense of humor, you'll see as we progress through this little journey.

Let's get started with the United States military, a good place to start, don't you think? Why, since the basic "WAR" in Iraq lasted about nine days!! Why are we still there, getting killed day in and day out, for really no other reason than the whole world is watching. They say we are trying to make Iraq into a Democratic Society!! Something I know first hand that they could car less about. You are not going to change history folks. I really do not care if we are there for twenty years, what happened before we were there is happening while we are there and it will be happening long after we are gone so tell me, what is the point of being there? It seems to me that we are just doing no more that pissing people off and turning them against the Americans, just the opposite of what I think you "believe" to be happening. How many lives does it take to say NO MORE!! We won, right? Then why are we still losing? Somebody please give me the answer to that one. We are fighting the War on Terror, thousands of miles away from us. Don't you think we should focus more on just our homeland security, you know, where we actually live, other than somewhere that other people live and we are the outsiders, maybe that's just my way of thinking, but I should know; I've been there. So, you are getting first hand information, not some skeptical view of some guy behind a computer desk somewhere, you are getting the bird's eye view from someone who has had his boots on the ground in some of the most dangerous places in Iraq, which really translates to some of the "most dangerous" places on our beautiful planet earth. So do not shake your head like I don't know what I am talking about, because I do, believe me. I know all too well!!

People have there own preconceived ideas on what is going on in the war, in both Iraq and Afghanistan. The media tells you just enough to make you turn your head and take a look. Let me ask a quick question. What do you think of when you see some catastrophic event plastered all over your television screen, internet or newspaper, do you think that is all that happened that day? Well, be honest, do you? Because if you answer yes, I have some beautiful beach front property in Montana!! If you believe that then you are really doing nothing more than fooling yourself, basically sticking your head in the sand and hiding! There is so much that goes on that no one ever hears about or sees, and you never will. Obviously if you have any connection to the conflict going on in either country you have had to have asked yourself at one time or another, why is it taking so long? Or, why are we still even there? If you have ever heard the phrase "we won the battle, but lost the war" or maybe you have heard just the opposite, either way, you have heard it I know. Well, that is basically it, we won the battle in no time flat, but we are still there, losing lives and billions of dollars a day! We won the battle but we are losing the war!! And even if we win the war, what have we won? It is not like we are going to send over several states to move in and live there. Or do you want to go live in Iraq or Afghanistan perhaps? I didn't think so!! Hell, the people that live there do not even want to live there; go figure! So why are we spending so much time, effort, resources and most of all money, for some place that we will not even inhabit? Why? You tell me because there are terrorists here! Yes, that is correct, but they are everywhere. I bet you would really be surprised to know how many people that live in the United States are on some kind or some agencies "Terrorist Watch" list. You would simply be amazed. But the blunt of our whole country's protection force is hundreds of thousands of miles away, fighting the "war on terror". So, just for curiosity, would you say the terrorists have an advantage to us being over there? Of course they do, just like football or baseball and basketball, the home team always has a little advantage. Sometimes it is huge and sometimes it is very small, but still there is some kind of advantage. Personally, would you rather say fight or have to defend yourself in your own backyard? Or, do you think you would have a better chance somewhere that your opponent knows every crook and cranny of, or somewhere you know every crook and cranny? See what I mean? You can have the most sophisticated weapons and vehicles in the world, but if you do not know where you are going to, to use them and how to get there!! What is the point? You are better off staying home, that's right, where you are comfortable and feel secure; makes sense does it not? Yet, we as a country are running all over the world, fighting and getting our asses handed to us! No more are the days of "we came, we saw, we overcame, we left"! We are still there, just hanging around spending billions of tax dollars and something way more important that that - "Human Beings" for no damn good reason at all. How long is this going to go on people? I am sure in another year or two we will be rushing to help somebody else, somewhere that is in some major crisis. You can mark my words, it is going to happen. It is in our history and as everyone knows, history does repeat itself. You'll see, the way the media is today you will already know it's coming, the "writing on the wall" so to speak, but it will happen again and again, we will just keep riding up on that white horse, until someone shoots us off and kills the horse! What a bad day that will be for everyone.

CHAPTER 2

Well, let's get to it shall we? Let's get in to the meat and potatoes behind this whole book. Why we will never win another war, or what you know as "winning at war". I think we will get started where pretty much everything in the world revolves around, yes you guessed it, "THE MONEY". Do you have any fragment of an idea about how much it costs every single day, twenty-four hours a day, seven days a week, three hundred sixty-five days a year? Well, each country that we are currently "fighting the war on terror", Iraq and Afghanistan, I would speculate that it costs somewhere in the neighborhood of about four million dollars a day, and that is not both; that is four million each, so let's just say eight million dollars a day. Do you actually know how much money that is? Now say we took one month out, thirty days. OK, thirty days times eight million dollars; that comes to twenty-four million dollars, if I have my sixth grade math correct. How much health care for elderly citizens or homeless citizens can you think could be helped with twenty-four million dollars. And, or course, I was just using health care as an example, but just think what twenty-four million dollars could contribute to, and that is one month out of the whole time we have been in Iraq and Afghanistan. Now, of course, all these are really guesstimates and approximates, but I am sure you get the jest behind it. Millions of tax dollars are spent every minute of every hour and the saddest part of all of this is that nobody really cares enough to put their foot down and stop it. I have been there, seen it and just would shake my head over and over. Some places in Iraq you would see military vehicles just parked, sitting, never moved, never used! And it looked like the line was a mile long. It was incredible. But you cannot really explain such things to someone who has never been there. They just cannot imagine such things, the billions that's right I said "billions" of tax dollars, just sitting around in some dusty, dingy, sandy ole' Iraq! Doing nothing more than just taking up space!! Not one damn thing more. Most all of the costs and spending is supposed to be some kind of public record!! But do you really think you really think you will ever see it anywhere? Would you know where to look? Or who to ask? No, you wouldn't, and that's the way they like it. Nobody knows a damn thing about nothing! Are your eyes starting to open just a little? I hope so, because we are barely scratching the surface right now. Oh, but we will!! Hopefully.

How about all the funds given to say Iraq to help get them more Democratic and able to secure themselves and police themselves! That's all a big puff of smoke. I do not get this whole, OK, get rid of Sadam Hussein, now let's help them build back what we just tore down taking them down. Will someone please explain that to me. Maybe I'm just slow or something, but why are we spending so much time, money especially and resources to build up something that we just tore town. It does not even sound logical when you say it out loud! That is because it makes no sense at all. OK, we got rid of one of the most infamous dictators in the history of the world but I guess that was not enough. Now it is like we are sympathetic for doing the right thing and we are trying to buy their acceptance! Why? Who cares? Do you? I don't. Should we have to "APOLOGIZE" for ridding the world of another Adolf Hitler or worse? I should hope not. We should have been happy with that and left well enough alone, but I guess that was not good enough; we have to play patty cake with them now and give them money, finances, equipment, oh, and of course the blood of the red-blooded Americans. No sense in it. It is total "BULLSHIT" when you start to think about it. And yes I know you see all these horrific stories about "life" in Iraq and how bad they have it, and how they are trying hard to be better. Bullshit!! In any town USA there are people who need help and probably live just as bad as some of the Iraq people and people just turn their heads and look the other way. It is a shame. We need to be helping someone at "HOME" before we help everyone else!! Of course, that is just my opinion, which does not amount to very much other than it is mine! Of course, wherever you look or whomever you ask the "actual" correct figure will never be known by anyone. The point is we are wasting so much money on NOTHING!! We are not getting a damn thing out of all of this. It would seem like if we were gaining something, like say oil for instance, would you not think gas prices should be like fifty cents a gallon? I sure do. Why shouldn't it be that way? There is more oil in Iraq than there are terrorists. I can tell you that for a fact. Where do you think they receive most of the money from? Donations? I don't think so. They sell black market oil and they make a huge profit from it. Nobody, and I mean "NOBODY" can account for how much actual oil is transported and exported or to whom or where or anything like that. Nobody really knows! I am sure if the real number was known you would not believe it. I know I don't. So, when you are at the gas station this week filling up the family car or your pickup truck, perhaps for the workweek ahead, think about this. How much more money would be in "YOUR" pocket if gas prices were say fifty cents a gallon? I have a good idea. A lot more! And

I am sure that everyone could use a little extra. I know I sure could. Sure, some of you are big budget people, very meticulous about spending. What say we change that two hundred fifty to four hundred dollars a month fuel bill to say somewhere in the neighborhood of like seventy five or even a hundred dollars. That would free up at least one hundred fifty dollars a month that you could spend somewhere else, possibly on an education fund for your child, something nice for the wife or maybe even that boat you have always wanted. Hey, now you might be able to afford it because, as you know, most motor boats run on gasoline also, so it would be cheaper to have yourself a little toy like that!! Sound good? Sure it does! Will it ever happen? Probably not. No, definitely not!! We have babied them, and when I say them, I am speaking of the Iraq and Afghanistan governments, so much that you cannot take anything from them now. We should have taken it from the very beginning!! As soon as we won!! Remember me mentioning before about us winning? But what did we get for that? I will tell you what we got. Are you ready? We got a big, fat ZERO!! That's right, not a damn thing. All the oil that we would ever need is right there in Iraq and nobody gives two shits about it!! I have seen it, tanker trucks lined up for miles to get filled up and when they do, seventy-five percent of them go who knows where. I don't, the military doesn't, the State Department doesn't, the Iraq government itself doesn't, so who does? Well I guess the best answer to that would be from "WHOEVER" is actually getting it. The terrorists perhaps? That would be my best guess or prediction. And people wonder how and why they can plan and execute such elaborate plans such as 9-11. Well, it is mainly because they have the funds to pull something catastrophic like that off!! You know something like that is just not put together overnight and to have such a large network like they do, they have to have money!! Money from black market fuel selling, that we should be confiscating anyway! There should not be any oil there to sell and steal, what have you. We should be taking it all for ourselves to make a better life for Americans!! Maybe if we made it easier for some people, we would not have such a homeless population that we do. People lose their jobs and cannot find work and they end up falling behind in their bills, especially mortgage or rent payments and before you know it they have nowhere to live and nowhere to go, so they end up on the street. How about this? We take over all of the oil refineries in Iraq, bring in unemployed Americans to manage and work in these refineries. People have jobs then they can pay their bills, keep their houses. All the oil exported would go to the United States, gasoline would be super cheap and energy costs would be super cheap. Any excess we could sell to the highest bidder and put that money into the healthcare system!! Sounds like a plan? I should run for office or something. I mean, we are already there in military terms, we won you know, so why shouldn't we be able to take a little for ourselves?

Believe me I have been there. We are doing nothing more than babysitting the Iraq government and security forces. Let's take what we want. They are not going to stop us! Remember; "WE" won and "THEY" lost, so why does this have to be so complicated. Just take what we need and make everybody happy!! Sounds too simple doesn't it? Yes it does, but this is just one of the reasons we will never win another war; because we are getting too soft. "HELL" it's war, should be not get something for winning? Damn right we should, anything and everything we want!! Hey, when they win the Super Bowl, don't they give them a trophy? See, if you win, that means you get something!! And supposedly we won!! You tell me does it look to you like we have won ANYTHING?

CHAPTER 3

Now, let's talk a little about giving things away, I mean besides the money. I think we covered the cost of this whole fiasco, but I am sure throughout this whole book the talk of money and finances will sure be referred to. I am not going to relate much to Afghanistan when I talk in this chapter, but I know it is the same as Iraq and I have personally seen these things in Iraq so I am sure the same can be said for Afghanistan. Here is another piece of the puzzle that no one person can put their finger on and tell you how and what resources have been given out over time. Here is my approximate guess. I'll say a "SHITLOAD"! I will say ninety-five percent too much! Of course that is just my opinion and yes, we have already determined how much that really matters, haven't we? But, really I am just trying to put all this in some kind of perspective. One of the examples I am going to use is about the Iraq security and police forces. Why? Because I know a lot about them and have seen it all up close and personal. So let me first say that all of the Iraq police and security vehicles are "supposedly" purchased through the Ministry of the Interior, which is funded by the United States government for the most part! They get brand new vehicles, trucks, cars, humvees for that matter, but they will not go along with any kind of maintenance plan. So what I am saying is, if they get brand new forty thousand dollar trucks and say after a month it breaks down, well then so be it. They do not fix it. Oh, sometimes they try to give the impression they are, but that is more of a show to pacify the United States military to think they are really trying to do something. It is actually quite funny to see them running around, taking pieces of a truck or car and not knowing what the hell they are doing! I have personally seen a brand new Dodge Ram 4x4 pickup truck, wrecked, turned over in the first four days it was there. The Iraq's just left it there sitting by itself, just left it and you know what their next sentence was? We want another one of those. We like those trucks! Well, I'll be damned, so does half of the male population. They would like to have a brand new Dodge Ram 4x4 pickup truck. But the big difference is, everybody else has to pay for theirs, not the Iraq police and security forces, they just give them another one and let them keep on truckin'.

The police stations and security stations in Iraq, the ones that you constantly see on television or the internet, getting blown up or bombed, some kind of major damage to it. Do you have any idea who is paying for all that? Both, what they just blew up and what they are going to put back to replace it? Take a guess. It is me, you, your next door neighbor, your cousin across the country, grandma and grandpa living on welfare!! It is all of us. We are working hard day in and day out so our families will have a roof over their heads and food on the table, and our hard earned tax dollars are being used in some of the most frivolous ways, most you could not even imagine in your wildest nightmares. I have seen the military spend hours and hours and hours of time building up some place that will more than likely be blown up before it is completely finished. And when I talk about building up and man hours, I am not talking about some kind of rag tag construction crew. I am talking about engineers, security forces, contractors, you name it, all being involved and all playing an important role twenty four hours a day seven days a week for however long it takes! A complete waste of time, money and resources, not counting in all the lives that have been lost in the process. That is the most devastating statistic of all!!

Let me keep on while I am rolling through the police and security forces. The Iraq police officers and security forces carry Glock 9mm pistols. The United States military carries Beretta 9mm pistols. Here is another question for you. Who pays for all of the Glock pistols carried by the Iraq police and security forces? Were they already there when the United States got there? Well, do you know the answer? Guess, come on; the United States State Department provides, furnishes, buys, whatever you want to call it, all of the Glock 9mm pistols that are currently being used by the Iraq police and security forces. Now isn't that just a kick in the pants. We are over there being shot at and killed at times by weapons that were purchased and given to them by our own State Department!! Does it sound crazy to you yet? That is what it is, plain and simple, total chaos, with no end in sight. I do not care who says what, it really doesn't matter. The dam has burst a long time ago, so to speak, and it is too late to try and recover from it. We need to just get the hell out!! But, by all means, let's give them some more "STUFF" before we finally leave. Oh, I am sure we will. That is in our nature now. That is our stereotype. It is too late to change all that. I know that and I am not Albert Einstein or something.

Let's say someone came to your house, said they were taking over, let you keep your house and they stayed in the yard. They escorted you to and from your job, so nothing could happen to you. They basically did your job for you. Your family would be protected twenty four hours a day while you were gone to work and when you got home, those people would still be in your yard protecting you and your family. And, of course, still once a month you would get paid, even though someone else was doing your job for you!! Then, maybe after a month or two in the yard, these people decided they wanted to build you a new, nicer, bigger house with all brand new furnishings of course, and they told you that you did not have to pay a thing, just live in it after they decided to leave. Now, does that sound horrible and horrendous? Hell no! It sounds pretty good, doesn't it? You damn right it does. All that is is a condensed, smaller version if you will of how it really is in Iraq for the average Iraq family. Sounds pretty good, I know, and it is, but nobody wants you to know that. All they want you to see is kids running around, crying, people walking around like they have nowhere to go. It is really not like that. Yes, some places are bad, but there again, there are some places probably in your city or town that are just like that, no better, no worse. So, do you think "ALL" Iraq or Afghan people have it terrible? I hope not. If you do, you must have skipped a few pages. Because most have it WAY better than you think they do or what the media portrays. Certainly it is not Shangri-La, but you would be surprised if you spent any time at all over there. And I used Iraq a lot during this segment because I have not personally been to Afghanistan, but did you know the number one export for Afghanistan is poppy. Most of you do, some do not. They use it to make heroin. So the country with the largest gross national product of poppy and probably supplies the rest of the world with eight five percent of all the poppy an heroin in the world, you don't think that there are just boat loads of money floating through there? You damn right there is. You might see some guy on television with all dirty clothes on and maybe three teeth, but he probably has a couple of million dollars stashed away somewhere, probably most likely in cash, buried in the ground or hidden in some barn or something like that. Believe me, it is true, but nobody wants you to see how bad they have it and how poor and helpless they are!! So we can help. That's right, give them "STUFF"!! Both places are the same, there is really nothing much different than one from the other. Both have been overrun by the United States military and others. Both claim to be on the side of the Americans and want to cooperate "COMPLETELY" with any thing the United States wants. Both claim corruption running straight down the country, from the highest ranking officials to the lowest man on the pole. Both say they want to stand on their own and try and give the impression that they are trying "SO" hard to do so. Both say they are working diligently to weed out Al Quida and the Taliban, so their countries will be peaceful and secure for all of their citizens. Both kiss the United States military and governments ass, to their faces and then constantly try and sabotage progress being made. Both countries are quote "losers" to us as far as war and conflicts go, yet we are still losing American lives every day in both countries. Both will be taken over by Iran and soon as the United States leaves in full force. Both are in no better shape than they were five years ago and both will still be in the same predicament five years from now. Both have been nursed and weaned by the United States military for so long that they know they do not even have to protect themselves because somebody is already trying to take care of that for them and doing a damn pretty good job. Both have received billions and billions of US tax dollars in the way of funds and resources for no other reason at all other than we were at "war". Both will play out this game of charades as long as they can. That only means that they have to do less than whatever they did before, no problem, right?

You see why they could care less if somewhere gets blown up or bombed. The United States probably gave it to them anyway and now all that means is they will get a new one. It is like a bunch of five year olds, spoiled rotten. They cry, we give! Over and over and over!! You get it?

CHAPTER 4

What's say, let's talk about strength for a few minutes. You know "Army Strong" and all that. You would probably cringe at some of the people you know or don't know that are fighting for you and everything you think of as freedom. Some of these people are probably old enough to be someone's great grandfather or grandmother!! I am not kidding. Eighty percent of what you think of about people being in the " Combat Zone" probably spend more than half their day inside of a dining facility, chow hall as it is called by the old timers. So, do not ever get some misguided information that Billy Jo, Bobby Sue never gets anything good to eat, that is why we have to send them snacks and food from home!! Because that is total BULLSHIT!! Most of the care packages that are sent usually end up in the local nationals hands as some point. So basically are you not only funding the "war" but actually sending food and snacks for the local nationals who in turn thank us by trying to kill us every chance they get. You are probably saying to yourself, NO WAY! Yes Way! I saw it every day, day in and day out. It was like kids in a candy store. Local nationals have Christmas about three or four times a week! The Americans give away that much crap to them. It is unbelievable. And by doing this so often, when they do not get it, they pout and whine and cry, like little babies. Even the children have become scam artists. A lot of the children I saw could probably make good money working on a Manhattan Street in New York City or downtown Los Angeles. They are that good at it. It was never how much you gave them of anything, they always wanted more and more and more!!! You could be giving away buckets of shit, but as long as you were giving it away, they wanted it and also as much as you had. I remember seeing children on the streets picking up candy and then just taking it somewhere to stockpile it. Then they would run back and grab more. If there was no more, then they would beg for more. A lot of guys say it as sad; I saw it another way, which you might say is pessimistic or bad, but after you have seen it over and over and over so many times before you just sort of look differently at it. And of course after you see the parents of these children sending them out to pray on the human emotions of soldiers, it sort of makes you sick to your stomach!! Makes you pissed off, you can imagine, so if you think I have a bad attitude, you are probably right, but a least you can see why now, can't you? I hope so.

But I am getting off track a bit. We were going to talk about strength. I started talking about food and we ended up here, but we will keep going now. Tell me, would you feel safe knowing the person directly in front of you or behind you watching your back could not even probably do ten pushups or ten sit-ups? How good would you feel relying on someone like that to be the one that was responsible for maybe saving your life? Or many lives for that matter? Do you think that you would like that? Probably not. I do not think anyone would. I didn't and I won't, that is probably a lot to do with why I doubt that I will ever go back to a combat zone unless the combat zone ends up right here in America. The United States military used to stress physical fitness, that was one of the most basic fundamental attributes. How many people have you heard about in your lifetime that "went off" and joined the military and came back a lean, mean, fighting machine? Well, that shit doesn't work like that any more. It is sad, very sad, to actually see how bad a shape some of these people really are in. And this may sound funny to you, but it is the majority of the younger ones who are in worse shape than say the old ten, fifteen year veterans. You would think that it would be the older ones, but it is just the opposite of that!! It is the younger newer soldiers who can not even pass the physical fitness test. I mean, the basic passing score. And yet that is who is defending you and everybody else. Kind of scary isn't it? If you don't know, then you really need to pay attention to each and every chapter in this book. I have seen some of the military that was at least one hundred pounds overweight. Now sure, you say everybody has a little extra weight on them and that well they are in a "War Zone". Who cares? I bet if you were riding along in a humvee through the streets of Bayji, Iraq and an IED went off, you would not want to rely on some person sitting next to you that took ten minutes to get in the truck and is sitting there eating candy bars while you are going down the road, do you? Now, doesn't that make you feel real good about your chances? Hell, they cannot take care of themselves so how the hell are they going to help you if you need it? They can't. They won't. They are not able to and that is the honest truth as cold as it sounds. I have seen so many guys and gals in recent years that cannot get promoted to the next rank and grade up all because they cannot pass the physical fitness requirements. You would think to yourself that the whole premise of "WAR" is fighting, and being strong would be a iatrical part of that, but that is not the why it is important anymore. It is more about numbers on a list and names on a roster, than it is actually being ready and able to accomplish the tasks given. I am sure that there are some parents out there that are reading this and they know good and well that their son or daughter did not have the physical make-up and stamina to withstand combat situations. And that is certainly not saying anything bad, it is that most parents really know what their children can or cannot do. They have been around them their whole lives and they know if they are athletic and physically able to do what is necessary, but saying all that they should not be there. It should not be about numbers folks. It should be about "WINNING" and being able to put the men and women in place to give us the best chance at doing just that, "WINNING". Now don't get the impression that I am saying "EVERYONE" is a fat slob or something. I am just looking at the big picture, the majority. The "majority" should not even be there to begin with. Some recruiters somewhere lied about something and just got Billy Joe, Bobby Sue pushed right through, when, in fact, , if they would do their jobs like they were supposed to, we probably would be able to rectify a lot of the craziness. A lot of times these military recruiters have a quota and it really does not matter to them exactly how they get to where they are supposed to be. It is not like they will ever see these people again. It very,

very seldom ever turns out that way, unless they know each other or something. Once they have that "John Hancock" on the dotted line, they could care less. The sooner you are gone, the better! As far as they are concerned. That's right, I called them "victims" because these people really have no clue as to what they are getting themselves into; none at all. And all the recruiter is going to tell them is basically what ever they want to hear, all good of course, nothing bad! We will just let them find out on their own, won't we? That's the way the recruiters feel about the whole thing, which is sad, but true. I know a lot of recruiters personally but it is basically the military version of a used car salesman! That's the way I look at it and again, yes, that is just my opinion, but it is also probably a little fact that you "DID" not know, but you should.

But everyone can make their own determination and I just hope this helps. One more thing that I want to add in here is that the media helps to give you the impression that they want you to have. The same goes on with the physical fitness that I have been talking about. When you see photos or highlights on television about the war and see soldiers walking down the street or talking to some of the Iraq children or something, you are not going to see some big, fat, overweight soldier on your television screen. You will see some young, in shape guy or gal and you say to yourself "boy they look like a "fighting machine", but let me let you in on a little secret, that is "BULLSHIT", because that is just for the cameras, no more, no less!! Just publicity, "Good" publicity and it usually goes a long way. But the day in and day out grind of war is being fought by more out of shape "kids" than anything else and it is sad to say, but at this point, that is about all we have! And those are becoming so scarce it is ridiculous! They cannot "Find" or even "Make" someone come to war. It is crazy. The ones they do force in to it do not want to be there to begin with, so why would they want to put out the extra effort to be and actually stay in shape? They are not and will not and that, my friends, is a sad statistic. I personally think that has a great deal to do with why we will never win another war. We are letting the basic backbone of the whole military concept, "strength", just fall by the wayside. It is way past the point of trying to fix it or change it and go back to the harder and stricter ways of doing things. And here is a tip, piece of trivia if you will, the rest of God's green earth is starting to realize and know this themselves. Why do you think we were challenged on our own soil that sad September morning? Because we have shown the rest of the world that we are vulnerable. Never before has the United States been attacked on their own soil since Pearl Harbor, but that is not exactly the same as New York City and Washington DC, is it? I do not think so, do you? If you do you will "REALLY" be surprised when we get attacked again, won't you?

CHAPTER 5

Now let's talk about the mindset or psychological basis for my so called theory. I plan to touch on both sides, so this chapter should be interesting. I am sure that this chapter will initialize some great long conversations and debates for everybody, which I think is great!! I hope you have your own opinion and express it sometime. You know that is what they call freedom of speech and to my best recollection, we have already fought a war to be able to do that, isn't that right? If I am wrong, please tell me. I "certainly" do not think I know everything or do I claim to be some kind of history major, but I think we can all agree that the United States fought the Revolutionary War to break away from England, to form our own government, a democracy, if I remember correctly. How can we force our ideals and beliefs on other people when we ourselves, a little over two hundred years old, were fighting for the same exact thing?

Also, I seem to recall something else in our past called the Civil War. Does anyone else remember that, or is it just me? That is when we were just at war with ourselves, no other countries or continents involved. We were just fighting amongst ourselves, killing each other!! Americans killing Americans! Does that possibly remind you of anything? Think hard a minute. Maybe when you hear on the news or internet that the Shiites are killing Sunnis or the Sunnis killing the Kurds, you say to yourself, that is terrible. Why don't you think we can stop it? Well, let me revert back a few sentences ago when I was talking about our own Civil War. Did you see England or Russia jump in to help and sort of play referee? No, of course you did not, because they could care less, but yet, in this day and time, the United States thinks that it is so powerful and mighty that they can just take care of everything!! Just ride in on that big white horse and save the day! Well, that just is not happening anymore. Those days are long gone and personally I do not think you will ever see it like that again, at least not in my our your lifetime, maybe our grandchildren or great grandchildren!! We , as a country and as an Armed Forces, are just not capable of that anymore and you know what? It is not that big a secret. The rest of the world knows that also. Why do you think we are in so many conflicts and wars? Do you think people just like picking on us? You do not see say China or Russia getting tested or challenged every other day, do you? No, you don't. Well, there has to be a reason for that folks. I don't think it is luck, do you? No, hell no! We have just shown to be so vulnerable in the last few decades it is ridiculous! Did anyone notice that the United States started to say "Get Challenged" just about the time the Vietnam War was winding down? That showed the entire world that we were vulnerable!! I am not going to say we lost, but we damn sure did not win! Depending on who you talk to as to whether we won or lost, but it doesn't really matter. What matters is that we lost all of those lives, basically for no good reason other than the simple fact that we were riding up on that "White Horse" and we got knocked the hell right off and have not been able to get back on it, or at least not like we should have. Countries and people see that, like Sadaam Hussein did. He had no problem confronting the United States, much less any other part of the world. He could care less. And, yes I know he is dead and yes I know that he made his own people suffer immensely, but the fact remains the same. He stood up and confronted the Untied States and yes, he is gone, but who won? We are still losing American lives in Iraq and Hussein has been dead for well over a year now. You tell me, who is winning? Or, who won? You might have to actually think about that now before you answer. At least I hope you think about it some before our answer!! Please, please look at the big picture and then tell me honestly, who won? I have been there, done that and I do not know exactly!! I know we did not win anything except for some more years of headaches, heartaches, broken hearts and huge, ""HUGE" budget deficits. What's the point to it?

You tell me, please!! I am waiting for you to answer. If you even have an answer you are probably either a politician or an alcoholic, or perhaps both. But of course that would only be if you were even honest with yourself! And we all know that if you are a politician that is pretty much out of the question!!

The mindset of playing the "Big Brother" protector or even "Savior" is not the reality anymore. The rest, or I should say most of the rest of the world just thinks we are busybodies, bullies if you will. Just going all over the world trying to solve everyone's problems and just make it a perfect world to live in. Well, I'm just here to say "NO WAY"!! No matter what you think you heard or know, the fact of the matter remains these countries do not want us here Sure they love to have all the resources, but they do not want us hanging around telling them what to do with it and who gets what. They want that to be left up to them and to this point it has not! Not anywhere. It seems to me that this resembles communism in some ways. We give them money, yet we tell them what they can buy or not buy. How do you think you would feel if, after a long forty or fifty hour week, your boss gives you your paycheck and he also gives you specific instructions on how you can spend it and where you can spend it? How do you think the idea of that sounds? And that is really the cold hard truth about it, because that is what really happens. There is no freedom of choice. You get exactly what you are told to get, nothing more, nothing less! Sounds like living in Russia or something, doesn't it? It does to me, at least that is the way I see it. Sure it does not play out anything like that in the media. The media can make you think any way it wants you to. I mean that is a big part of their job, to persuade you to feel about one particular thing, one way or the other. If they do, then obviously they have done a good job at what they do. To put this in perspective or an example you can correlate with. Think about the political elections. When a newspaper comes out and endorses one candidate or the other, that always is such a big deal. Some people actually look at which newspaper endorses which candidate so they will know which way they want to go!! The truth? Of course it is, so there is what I am talking about when I say the media tries to persuade you and they do, you just might not know it. So, if that same newspaper you trust so much tells you how much good we are doing and so on and so forth, you will more than likely believe that also! You say you won't, but the fact is you already do and do not even know it. Kind of scary isn't it? What else have you been "persuaded" to believe? That we won the war? That we are making a difference? That all the lives have been lost for a good reason? That your sons and daughters are doing the right thing? That you are any safer in your own home than you were seven years ago? Each person will have to answer these questions individually, and I am sure everyone will have all different answers and that is good, I guess. I don't know. Only you can be the judge of that. When I first started this chapter I said we were going to talk about psychological issues and that there would be a lot of discussion after you have read this chapter and I hope that is all true.

How much now do you really truly in your heart and mind believe? And how much do you think you have been persuaded to believe? Some politician or military person will get on television and tell you that "we are making a difference and that you can see changes". Really? Where? I have not seen any changes in years, just the same old song and dance routine. The only thing you can see in black and white is that millions, I should say billions of tax dollars are being spent every year and there is NO change!! Nothing!! Oh, a good luck story here and there, but that is really about it. Nothing with any significant, long lasting effect on anybody, certainly not us, because remember, we do not live there and the people who do cannot hardly stand it waiting for us to get the hell out of there!! Hell, I have spoken to people that said that "they had it better under Sadaam than they do now". So what does that statement tell you? That we are making some great contributions or differences? Hell no, it doesn't. All it does is give you some insight to how much these people hate us and want us gone. And it is deep seeded hatred too, all the way to the bone! From the youngest to the oldest and visa versa, they all hate us. Yet some of the military gets so friendly with some of the local nationals. They give them extra supplies, extra money, free medical at times, places to live and work. The military does all that for the local nationals yet we have so many people in the United States that are not afforded any of that. Why is that do you suppose? I sure cannot figure it out, but I guess we have been 'persuaded' enough to think that in our country, so I guess we can help all these other citizens of foreign countries, but we will not help our own. Somebody tell me when did we lose compassion for our own citizens in need? And become every other countries' Mother? Somebody want to give me the date for that? I wish you would because I'm sure we could make it in to some kind of holiday or something!! You know another holiday where we can take off from work and do nothing, barbeque and beer or something like that and maybe fireworks at night. You know, celebration of the day the United States became the world's Mother. Another holiday. I can't wait. I just hope they put it in the summer months so everyone can celebrate it on the beaches, you know, like Memorial Day or the Fourth of July! That sounds good, right?

Worldwide Police work, just hanging around.

Normal Iraq Government building.

Police Station in good shape.

Most popular view of Iraq.

The man, the myth, the legend.

Executive washroom!

Brand new police station!

Another one bites the dust!

Busiest place in Iraq.

American Made!

CHAPTER 6

Now let's talk about the "civilian" connection that is attached to all this bullshit!! All the companies from all over the world who are making huge profits off of all these wars. There are so many people that are making "SO" much money as long as the "War" keeps on going, it is unbelievable. Personally I am anxious to see what all these people are going to do about job and income once the "WARS" are all over. I am sure a lot of them will never have to work again if they are smart with their money, but of course most are not! Most of the dumbasses I know spend more time spending it than they do making it, which only means they need more! It is like a drug addict or something. They get some and it is never enough. They need more.

Now, tell me can you recall any other war or conflict that there has been so many "private entities" involved? I know I sure haven't! I cannot recall seeing old footage of World War II or the Korean War and seeing all these "private contractors" running around with the military.   All it is basically is legalized mercenaries, some of whom know what to do and most who do not, but that is just my opinion on the whole deal, but I have been there. So, I think I should know, don't you? Well, maybe you don't, but keep reading and you will maybe have to rethink your views. What I can attest to is that I have seen thousands of people paid billions, yes, billions or dollars over the span of years during and especially after the war was so called, OVER!! And for the most part, it is pretty much the same people and the same companies who, through some unknown affiliation seem to get "ALL" the government contracts!! Well, well, if it isn't the "Good ole boy" system gone global

I don't know what is! It is the same thing you hear about every day in the United States. Some company gets all the contracts for some city or town, always has and probably always will. The same shit happens in the "COMBAT" zone. The same companies get all the contracts no matter who ever bids against them. You see the same brand of snacks all the time. You see the same brand of computers all the time, except for personal computers. You see the same brand of batteries, You see the same brand of cereal. I can go on and on with examples, but I think you get the picture by now don't you? At least I hope you do! Why, you say? Because it is the damn truth!! But that is what I am trying to get through and show you. It is not "WAR" anymore, like you have known in the past. It is not about who is right or wrong, or even who is a diabolical maniac. It is all about the "BUSINESS" of war now! It has turned into big business. And the Ball is rolling so fast now and there are so many hands in the cookie jar than it will never stop, at least in our lifetime, it will not. It is not about beliefs, politics or even the most used cause, religion, it is all about big business. And the best business going today is "WAR". The business is of war and it is a good one folks.

Now, you might be saying to your self what does all this have to do with us not ever winning another war. Well it looks to me like we do not want to. We want to always go to war, but we never want to leave. I attribute this a lot to how lazy the American public has become. With technological advances and all of the new gadgets and gizmos, too many to mention. We are always looking for the "EASY" way out of everything. How to get more for doing less!! That, my friend, is the "New American Dream". Remember you heard it here first! The New American Dream is to get more, for doing less. And we are getting so good at it over the past few decades you just don't realize. You have to sit back and look at the big picture. If you would, you would see what I am talking about. Some of you probably already see it, you know, you see it yourself. You see it everyday, professional athletes, movie stars and musicians all make extravagant amounts of money for the most part for small amounts of work. The average movie we'll say takes sixteen weeks make, that is four months. I do not know, I am just trying to make a point. OK, sixteen weeks or work some actors or actresses make anywhere from five to fifteen million dollars and then usually some type of proceeds from the gross. So am

I right? Sure I am. Everyone knows this because it is so widely publicized, so it is no big secret. But do you know how much money say, Blackwater, makes for providing security for diplomats in Iraq? Of course you don't and you never will. So what is the difference between that and say what George Clooney made for his last picture? Nothing other than nobody wants you to know a thing about anything so they can keep the gravy train running right on down the tracks to nowhere! No where except some certain people's bank accounts, which most are off shore anyway, in a tax free environment, so what extravagant amounts they are getting is like having it doubled because there is no tax taken out folks! That's right. Your tax dollars are being taken out to fund wars where the main participants are not even paying taxes anyway! Now how many of you out there actually knew that? Just a handful I bet. Now are you starting to see the light at the end of the tunnel? Now are you starting to realize why I say that the business of "war" will never stop? There are too many people's jobs and livelihoods that one hundred percent depend on the business of war never stopping!! And it won't, I don't care how many lives are lost. The profit margin has become so big and so large scale, it cannot "EVER" stop. Sounds pretty gloomy doesn't it? I personally think it does, but that's just me. What do I know? Not much? Or maybe more than I need to! I guess you can make that determination. I am just trying to give you all the factors that come in to play when I say we will never win another war. You might think that is a bold or brash statement, but you have to look at some of the reasons I say what I do. Of course I am talking about your children, your children's children and so on and so forth, future generations. And of course when I speak of future generations, I just hope that is makes it that far. If the civilians have anything to do with it, it will go on forever. As long as somebody is making money and getting theirs! They could care less about the ramifications of endless war or combat. All they know is it is a way for a very small group of people to become extremely wealthy, all at the expense of others. And that is not some fantasy or something. That is cold hard reality.

I am sure you read or hear about every other day how much this war is costing taxpayers. That is you and me and everybody else. The fact is we are funding a war just so some people and companies can get fat off of it. It is a shame!! We have been in Iraq since 2003. Now really don't you think by now if we were going to make some kind of difference we would have? Even a small part? But we have not and will not. We will only do what is allowed and no more and sometimes less!! A lot of military are handcuffed by political powers that be and just are not allowed to do what is necessary until in most cases it is too late!! I mean Iraq really has no military. They have what is left of the IA - Iraq Army and the majority of them still hate and resent the Americans so why should they want to conform and take our advice? They could give a shit less about what we think or about what we "want' them to be like!! They just would rather spend their time trying to kill us. But, I am getting off on a little tangent. Let me regroup and get back to the civilian connection. If there were no wars or conflicts going on somewhere in the world what would all of these companies that manufacture and sell weapons and ammo do? Would they just go belly up? If nobody is killing anybody, would it not seem so? So they have a huge, huge piece of the pie! The more killing, the more money for them, and the longer it lasts only means profits for months and years to come!! And don't think they are not protecting how much they will be making in a year or two, because they are and they can. They know that these things will just continue to drag out and when it fizzles out, there will be a brand new one getting ready to start. Watch and see for yourself. It happens that way every time. Just sit back and think about it for a while. Have you ever, since you have been born, known there to be "Peace on Earth" with nobody fighting or at war with nobody else? I cannot, but maybe you can, but you would probably have to be oh, four thousand years old!! Anyone out there that old? If anyone answers yes, then you should not be reading this book. You should be writing one. As good long one, OK? I will read that one myself. But seriously as long as you can remember, some group of people have been at odds with another, forever, throughout history. And they say history repeats itself and I am one to go along with that belief. After you see it over and over again, and you watch and see all the significant players in the game. And what that is really turning into is some kind of sick, political "GAME". It does not matter really who wins or loses anymore, because that is all inconsequential to the overall objective, which is to make people a lot of money for how ever long you can, before someone actually finds out.

I thought that this would be a good spot to throw in a little "WAR" trivia. In Iraq they have water distilleries that manufacture, purify, bottle and distribute water through Iraq. You can imaging with the heat getting up to one hundred forty degrees some days, how important water is to the whole "Big Picture" when it comes to Iraq. Well, you know who owns most of these plants in Iraq? Go ahead and guess. No, it is not Oprah or Donald. It is the Vice-President of the United States, Dick Cheney!! That's right, the Vice-President of the United States owns water plants in the poverty ruined country of Iraq!! Well, go figure. So, how much do you think he has made during those five years of "War" in Iraq? Probably enough for all of us to be living comfortably for the rest of our days. But little things like that make you start to realize, hey, I think this guy is on to something. I can see why nobody wants us to leave Iraq. It will cost too many people too much money!! And they are just not going to have that now, are they?

CHAPTER 7

Ever since the first World War the United States has had several allies and other countries that they can count on, especially when the going gets tough! But in this day and time the allies of the United States patience are wearing very thin. I can tell you from experience and having boots on the ground in Iraq, that not everyone and every country are happy we went there "initially" and are certainly not happy that we are still there!! I do not care what you might think you see on CNN or Fox News. We are pretty much in these "wars" or "conflicts" if you will all on our own. And folks, let me be the first one to say that we are not as nearly as strong militarily as you or your next door neighbor would like to think. I know it sounds bad, and believe me, I am the first one to be pissed off about this, but it is just the cold, hard truth. And it certainly is not easy to swallow. But getting back to our allies patience towards us, let's talk about this for a while.

A lot has been in the media about Great Britain's turning these provinces back under the Iraq government control. But as everyone has seen in the first quarter of 2008, these provinces, especially Basra, has seen an increase of violence and an escalation of attacks on the United States military that is still in and around that region. While all this was going on, did you once year Great Britain say they were sending more of "THEIR" troops back to help? No, you did not! That has never been mentioned at all, only political jargon about completing the" OVERALL" mission. Nothing about sending troops back in to help! Why do you think this is? I am asking you, you tell me. I think, personally, they are tired of it and do not want to lose anymore lives or spend anymore money on a useless cause!! Of course that is just my personal opinion and everyone has to make their own decision. But again, I reiterate that there has been no decision to send any British troops back, has there? I sure have not seen or heard anything about that, and I am sure something like that would be news worthy, don't you? Something like that would be plastered all over the television stations in every way, shape and form!! But you have not heard anything like that have you? And you will not, because the United States allies are fed up with the war and with us pretty much!! They certainly do not want to lose anymore than they already have!! For no good reason!! And who can blame them!!

Now, for the record, Great Britain is not our only ally, but I am sure you know that Germany, Russia and several other countries are what are considered now to be our allies, in some circles, but you have not seen or heard about any of there troops engaged in any conflict, especially not anything dealing with any "War on Terror". What does that tell you? Apparently they do not have any problems with terrorist or anybody else for that matter! Only with the aspect of helping the United States whenever it calls or "Cries Wolf" if you will. Our allies are starting to realize that "WE" could actually not be right all of the time. Maybe they do not want to help the bully out this time!! They just want to be like the citizen on the street and not get involved. They want to just walk on by like they did not see or hear anything at all!! Sound familiar? Sure it does. It is the old common adage that if you don't get involved, then nothing bad can happen to you. And that is absolutely true some of the time. Key word here is "SOME" of the time if you do not get involved then nothing will happen. Then again "SOME" of the time it really doesn't matter if you get involved or not; something bad is going to happen anyway! No matter what you do, get involved or don't get involved, something bad is going to happen anyway! But most of our allies feel at this point if they "do not" get involved, especially with things to do with the Untied States military, that they have a better chance of not having anything bad happen to their country and their population. And at this point you cannot blame them. Everyone watches day in and day out how the Americans are being attacked by every possible means available, in both Iraq and Afghanistan and a few other places that do not make the front pages just yet, but you will hear and see about them in the future! Just remember that you read something about that a long time ago and that you had a little bit of a "heads up" on what was going on from this little paperback book you happen to read on the plane or train one day on the way home from a vacation or work perhaps! Don't let some new news just sneak up on you. Pay attention, have at least a little clue about the rest of the world because I am here to tell you that it "ALL" will affect you somewhere, somehow, sometime!! Maybe not next week, next month or even next year, but sooner or later what is going on worldwide will affect each and every one somehow!!

That is why I am bringing up the topic of allies and how big a role that is going to play in present, as well as or even more in the future. One reason is you see our allies backing off, as I mentioned earlier, protecting their own and protecting their best interest. At this point, "WE" as a country have somehow gotten away from this concept. "We" seem to be in the business or protecting everyone else and doing for everyone else, rather than protecting and preserving our own way of life. We are so busy trying to push our Western Democratic ideals and beliefs down the Iraq peoples' throats, we have lost sight of our own ideals and beliefs. Things such as our youth, education and most recently our own economy which is probably as bas as it has been since the Great Depression of the thirties. I have been waiting to see all of the brokers on Wall Street just jump out of the window at the end of the day one Friday as they did on Black Friday!! Only this time, it will probably be covered by ESPN like type of Olympic event call something like "broker diving" or "broker freestyle". But why, as the most powerful and prosperous nation in the world, do we fail to take care of "OUR" own and let people lose their jobs, houses and even lives because we fail to help our own. Instead, we are in the fifth year of spending billions and billions and even more billions on a nation that does not even care one way or the other!! They could care less at this point!

Now mind you that I am not saying that we as a "COUNTRY" have no friends. I am just saying that the rest of the free world is getting fed up with all of our bulling tactics! And the only ones that it will affect, hurt if you will, in the long run is ourselves. I am just trying to emphasize a little about our allies and so called friends, if we lost them in part or in full we will probably never get them back! At least we will probably never really be able to rely on them as we did in the past. You can only cry "WOLF" so many times before everyone gets tired of it and quits running to our rescue or just to help you. And let me be the first to fill you in on this folks. In this day and time, with our military spread so thin and spread out, we are not the power in the eyes of the rest of the world that of course we once were!! Nowhere close to that and the sooner everybody comes to grips with that, the better off we will be. Personally I do not think we could withstand any more conflicts, especially right now!! For the main reason our military is spread out so much over the whole world! Sure there are a tone of troops in Iraq, everybody knows that, but how about in the rest of the world? South American, Africa, China and Japan; places like that. If the bases we have in some of these countries were attacked, they would be on their own for a long time before the "Calvary" could get to them. That translates into the loss of more American lives and I, for one, think there has been way too much of that already!! WAY too much! But, let's just for the sake of this argument, say that the Marine base in Japan was attacked. Do you really think, in all honesty, that say Great Britain would rush to help? Do you think they would send troops at the drop of a dime to come help? Maybe? Maybe NOT! I personally feel like they would sit back and wait to be asked to help, and probably thirty years ago, would not blink an eye and would be right there, no matter what! I am telling you, we are wearing down the patience of our allies and we really do not want to do that because "we" cannot win it on our own anymore. We need the help and we need to keep up our alliances with other powerful nations, not piss them off and push them away, but try to be more of a team player instead of the third grade bully that always has to have his way!!

One of the most common phrases you hear in any combat zone is "be flexible", because so much can change so fast and so often. But we never seem to take our own advice. We are just focused on one particular mission and yes, it is an important one, probably the most important one we will ever have, which is National Security, but we ourselves need to be flexible. Whatever your stance is on the war, whether you are for it or against it, or maybe you were for it at one time and now have gone against it or even visa versa, I have been there, boots on the ground and I just have to say that it is not working. Now don't get me wrong, some things are better, some are worse and a lot is the same as it always will be! So why can't we be flexible? We tell everyone that, so why can't we? I sure to not know. We should sit back and listen to our own advice sometime. It is almost like the crazy parent that keeps telling his kids "do what I tell you to do, not what I do". It is about the same basic premise, just on a much larger scale.

The whole bottom line to this chapter about our allies and how it pertains to the theme of the whole book is that "we" are just not as strong and powerful as we used to be. I, more than anyone, would wish that would change, but there are so many aspects that are involved with that and I hope this book is bringing some of these to light. I wish it was like it was fifty to sixty years ago when no one and no country dared to be at odds with the United States. Back then we were respected and revered the world over, or at least as much of the world that was known then. Now it is like every country, no matter how small in statue, wants to challenge us and try to stand up against us and even certain groups, Al Quida and certain people, Osama Bin Laden, want to attack us on our own soil. You would think that would be a wake up call for everyone!! But is seems it was just a wake up call for a few!! But in this complex, chaotic and violent world we inhabit now, we cannot do it alone ANYMORE!

CHAPTER 8

"Army Strong". That is the most recent slogan for the United States Army. Sounds good doesn't it? But it is just like any other slogan or advertisement, just like some high end Super Bowl commercial, sounds good but it is really not true. The United States military is hurting for people, good raw your recruits. It seems like they would rather join a street gang or sell drugs. Anything other than joining the military. That's sad and horrible to say, but those are just the cold, hard facts. Hell, three fourths of most of the reserve soldiers and National Guardsmen that are deployed work in some type of recruiting job back in the states, but they must not be doing too well because they end up over in Iraq and Afghanistan trying to accomplish tasks and carry out missions that they have no training, experience or even a "CLUE" on how to make it happen. Yes, I certainly applaud them for being there and yes, I worked along side of several different groups, but on more than one occasion I, "ME", myself had to make decisions that could affect the lives of a lot of people, split second decisions that had to be made, and had to be made right then! Thank God I made all of the right decisions. Experience and training helped, but luck also played a big part or the whole process!! But when you start to count on luck in a combat zone, then that should tell you right there that you are definitely on the wrong track!! When luck starts becoming a factor in combat operations and even combat operational planning, then it is time to reassess the whole scenario. Do you agree or disagree? Either way you feel, that's fine. Everyone is entitled to their own opinion, but frankly it is a little scary to deal with the whole "War on Terror" with luck!! Don't you think? And luck has helped a lot of these Reserve and National Guard soldiers make it back home safely to their families and loved ones, which is the best scenario that I could ever possibly hope for. I want everyone to come home safely and in one piece and if I have to pray for luck, I will! Whatever it takes to help bring our troops back safely! I will be the first to say I was lucky myself and feel blessed to have made it through some of the bad situations and spots that I was personally in and make it back home!! To be able to sit and write this book and to try and help educate and inform the American people makes me feel "LUCKY" just to be able to sit outside, nothing to listen to except the birds singing, trying not to think about getting mortared or blown up. Yeah, I feel lucky as hell!! Wouldn't you?

Now back to the recruiters for a few minutes. A recruiter's basic job is to actually go out and find candidates, young people that would make good soldiers. Most of the recruiters I know just sit in an office somewhere, talk on the phone and play on the computer. When they do speak to someone in person, they never really tell them the whole story and more times than not the reason they do not is because they have never been there themselves! They have kissed some ass or something to get this cushy, easy, recruiter job. Most do not have any combat experience at all. Now let me say that this is not "EVERY" recruiter, just the majority. There are a few good ones, just like there are good soldiers, good policemen and good politicians!! Yeah, good politicians. That's a good one, right? But, yes I have seen and known some great recruiters, but these are not nearly enough. They have changed so many of the policies and rules over the years, especially recently, because they cannot get anyone to join. And all this is starting to take effect now. Active duty guys just signing on for eighteen months, doing the bare minimum and getting out. Reserve and National Guardsmen not reenlisting or hard shipping to get out just to get out because they do not want to be deployed overseas or redeployed overseas. The age limit to actually join the Armed Forces has been raised which is good for several reasons. The most important being that you might be able to get someone that is mature enough to deal with all of the mental anguish that goes in to being in a combat zone and being far, far away from your family and friends. That is a "HUGE" problem with the younger, immature soldiers, but they really cannot help it, being thrown right straight into the middle of "HELL" and they are eighteen, nineteen, twenty year old kids who haven't even gotten to experience much of like yet anyway and then by tossed right into that shithole! You cannot expect them to act like experienced combat veterans because they are not! They are just young kids, impressionable young adults, who, for one reason or the other, have made the decision to join the military for whatever reason.

But the point that I am trying to make here is this; the attrition rate and retention rate is atrocious. I will use the following example to just try and simplify what I am actually trying to say. Let's take the Indianapolis Colts, just because they are usually one of the top football teams in the National Football League. They have some great superstar players like Peyton Manning, Marvin Harrison and a few more. If they just kept the same team year after year, without adding new players, not replacing the ones that retire, get injured and have to quit, then real soon they would start to go down hill!! The superstars would start to take a toll of their bodies and their talents, mentally and also they would begin to wear down. They would find out no matter how good "they" were, if they did not have good support and constant new and improved players around them, that "they" could not carry the load all alone. The team would begin to lose and the superstars, as bad as they wanted to, could not do anything to stop it!! Same goes for the soldiers. Picture the United States military as a team, a great team with superstar soldiers all over the world, but just like my example, many are leaving, getting out, frustrated, tired, too many reasons to name and we are not replacing them with anyone! Because nobody wants to do it and just like the sports team that goes on a downward spiral, so will our United States military!! And do you know what that will lead to? Yes, just like the sports team example. It will lead to losses! And in this day and time we cannot afford to lose anything because if the United States military loses, that means each and every American citizen will lost and I certainly do not think that any of us want that! I know I don't.

I know personally that I will do whatever it takes not to see that happen. Hell, by the time this book comes out, I, more than likely, will be right back in the middle of the combat zone myself. You might think that is crazy, but personally I feel obligated, for some strange reason. I guess my personal views overshadow my own objectivity. I remember speaking with my sister on the telephone before I went to Iraq one time and I remember her saying "I cannot believe you are going over there. It's crazy over there". My reply to her was "who do you think has a better chance to survive over there, me or your nineteen year old son?" She paused a moment and said "well, you of course. You have the experience and training, as well as the mental toughness, but it is still dangerous". And I said "yes, I know, but better me go than your son's" and she said "yeah, you are probably right". And I was right and I did help, and yes probably by the time you are reading this I will be back overseas somewhere, Iraq, Afghanistan maybe even in the Sudan somewhere. Who knows at this point. I don't. Hell, I might even be in Iran, because I'm sure we will be there before too long.

But, maybe if some people that are reading this book might ever take up the cause and join the military yourself, that would be great. And do not get me wrong on this. The United States military is a great career. You do not have to be in the Army or Marines. There are other branches as well. The Air Force, Navy and Coast Guard are all components that are combined together to make up our Armed Forces. Just pick one.

The theme of this book is about why we will never win another war and here I am recruiting for the military. The reason for that is I do not want to get it to that point. "I" personally do not like to LOSE!! How about you? This book is just a source of reference as to why we will never win another war. Maybe together we can all change that. I am not letting out some super secret CIA information. All I am doing is telling and speaking about some cold, hard facts. A lot of basic common knowledge that you have never even heard or thought about. But a lot of times if someone reads something, they are more inclined to believe it and remember it, which I hope is the case here!

Recruiting is a hard job, I will grant you that, but did you know that as we speak you can have a felony conviction and still be accepted into the Armed

Forces? Yes, that's right. They are now willing to grant a waiver to some felonies, certain ones that do not involve violence and things of that nature and you can still be accepted in the military!! And they still are having a whale of a time trying to get people to enlist. You would think that would open up the door and the line would be around the corner, wouldn't you? Well, it's not. They still cannot get anyone to enlist, just because "NOBODY" wants to go! Nobody wants to do the right thing anymore. They want to stay home and sell dope or join a gang, then sell dope! I have an idea; listen to this! How about we start recruiting from our state prisons and institutions? We as taxpayers are feeding, housing, clothing and educating these prisoners for years and years. Every state in the Union I know has a problem with prison overcrowding so why not recruit some of these people? I am sure some would jump at the chance to start fresh and new! With a new career, new job, who cares if the work release is in Iraq or Afghanistan. They are all criminals over there anyway. Sounds like a perfect fit to me! Any thoughts? Sure would make recruiting easier!!

CHAPTER 9

Helping out here, sending troops here, sending aid there, sending supplies over there!! It goes on and on and on. Yet, in the United States thousands are losing their jobs every week! More people, families than ever before have no medical insurance. Americans are losing their homes at the rate of tens of thousands a day!! The price of gasoline is climbing as we speak. Who has ANY idea when it will bottom out? Yet, we try to play big, bad, "Protector" all over the world. We are spreading it all to thin. We need to huddle up and regroup, if you will. We cannot afford to let our "OWN" resources that made us this strong to begin with just get whittled down to nothing. We need to do something to change this roller coaster that is heading straight down, with not much track left.

You have got millionaires in Congress arguing about raising the minimum wage! How ludicrous does that sound to you? I know many of you out there are just thousandaires, like myself. You know, just making enough to get by and if you are lucky, have a little ends meat left over at the end of the month so you might be able to splurge a little bit.

But how about all these soldiers, reservists and guardsmen especially, who come back from serving their country only to find out that there are really no jobs available for them and most start to feel like they had it better where they were than they do when they get back. Personally, I felt like that a lot. At least what you have to yourself, you could protect it as "GOOD" or as "BAD" as you wanted to. But is was yours and nobody was going to walk up to your tent and put a foreclosure sign on it and lock it up!! That just was not in the cards. Now, of course, it could get blown up at anytime, but hey, we already knew that. That's the norm. Just part of the deal. And I did not see or hear about anyone waking up in the morning, walking outside and seeing their humvee or other military vehicle gone! Repossessed by the "REPO" man! Nope, just didn't have that happen. Not part of the program, "thank you". Never happened and never will, but it happens every day in the states. So, part of what I am trying to get across is that the economy is getting so bad and more and more Americans are being affected every single day, that people are going to start forgetting about and even start not worrying about the men and women that are all over the world fighting the "War on Terror" on a daily basis. And when they start forgetting, then they will sure start not supporting!! Because that would be the obvious next step. Do you agree? Maybe, maybe not.

An example for you. Say you lost your job and or course your insurance coverage went with the job, so you lost that also. Unexpectedly your son or daughter is diagnosed with some type of catastrophic illness and needs an operation. But also this point you cannot afford it, so do you think you really care about how much the new military vehicle costs to make? Hell no you don't. All you know is that you could use that money to pay for your child's operation and rightly so!! But that is how the economy back in the United States affects the way the "war" is fought and also how the whole situation is interpreted. And if you do not think this has an effect on the overall mission and more importantly mission "Accomplished", you are living in the stone age or something!! Or your head under a rock perhaps?

When the price of gasoline just keeps going up, up and away!! If the "average" American knew how much crude oil that the Iraq oil refineries produce while being guarded by the United States military, then shipped to who knows where, there would probably be rioting in the streets!! It would look like something straight out of a movie! A giant wave of people massed together, in a frenzy! And all this over something that is within our grasp and means, but we fail to utilize it or even contemplate it! I guess those decisions are made by people a lot higher in the food chain than either you or me. Maybe I can be one of those people one day. One of those who gets to make the decisions. Decisions that affect everyone. No, I doubt it. I tell the truth too much for that! I am sure I will never get in that position. What a dream! Wishful thinking, I guess.

The basic point I am trying to get across is this! Milk reaching almost five dollars a gallon! Gas? Who knows "how" high at this point and so on and so forth. So why can't we take care of our own problems first? Instead of spending all of this money for things for other countries, yet "OUR" own country is in bad shape?

And, of course, now with everyone and their brother in the world having cable television and high speed internet access, the whole world knows exactly what is going on in our backyard! They get to watch it first hand, like a bad soap opera that just keeps going! One terrible circumstance or dilemma after the other!! I just do not want to see what we know now as the most powerful nation in the world get cancelled! Do you? You at least have to give me that. When I got back from Iraq, I was real nervous being around a large group of people, but pretty much I have been that way most of my life, so it only escalated it, not created it! That is just a personal thing.

CHAPTER 10

Several people have brought several things to my attention during the course of my travels, especially after I had come back from Iraq. At this point, I would like to share some of those observations and just some of my feelings with you. When I first arrived back, a lot of people stated that I seemed very angry and I probably did, and for some part probably still do!! I am sure that you see a lot of that come out in my writing, but hey, that is just me!! I am sorry if you do not like it, but one thing that I will have to say for the record is that I was truthful and told the stories and explained the circumstances to the best of my ability! You at least have to give me that. When I returned from Iraq, I was real nervous being around a large group of people, but for the most part, I have been that way most of my life so having been through what I have been through and having seen what I have seen only escalated it, not created it!! To see and hear about people losing their jobs and losing their homes only reiterated my feelings about being angry and being sad, of course. I am a very proud and professional person and that has a lot to do with why I feel the way I do and I am sure that it affects what I write and say, but that is alright. To get back from being gone thirteen months and to see people that you have not seen in a while say "So, what are you doing now?" Brings it all to perspective. I know each and every person has their own life, problems and whatever, but sometimes I have to just step back and relax and hold my tongue because I just want to scream and yell at them and tell them that "there is a big world out there" and they should "get in the game"!! But I don't because I have learned that most people do not care much about anything else other than what actually affects them and the people close to them!! If it does no have anything to do with them, they do not want to hear it, see it, read it or talk about it.

I felt many times like I would rather be back in Iraq in the combat zone rather than being home in the States!! Does that sound crazy to you? Knowing you can get shot at and blown up on a daily basis, yet you would rather be there than "HOME" in the United States!! I feel like that a lot, even to this day. Maybe I could do more? Maybe I could make more of a difference? Help a lot more people? Possibly save more lives? I live with these thoughts every day. Some professional people that I have spoken with stated "I should be proud to know" know that I have accomplished so much; awards, letters, recommendations!! I should be satisfied, yet I am not most of the time. I suppose that is just my own professional work ethic and moral code, but that is me and I will always be this way.

I have even had people tell me how to write! To write something, then read it and then blah, blah, blah!!! Well, I never said I was Ernest Hemmingway and for all the people telling me how I should write, my question to you is why don't you write one? Then I can go from your example!!

People keep telling me this and that. I should have done this, I should have done that, I should do this!! All I am trying to do is provide the average person with some education and some insight. If you enjoyed any part of this book or smiles at some point or maybe shook your head at some point, then I feel like I have accomplished what I set out to do!! And, maybe that certain person will read this and will be in the position to actually make some improvements. I would really get a kick out of that!

But if you have liked or not, agreed or not, I hope you know that I have done the best I could! And that is all that can be asked for and all that "SHOULD" be asked for!! In closing, I would say that I am proud of what I have done and would greatly do it again! Why? Because I am a proud American!! God Bless Everyone.

AFTERWORD

I hope that you have not taken anything in this book personally. What it really is about is something to really think about long and hard? I am not trying to belittle or speak about anything or anyone with some of agenda. All I have done is present some facts that everyone should take a cold hard look at some time and realize that that is a part of our world every day, and will be a part of our children's and their grandchildren's world for years to come . I want to see the United States

Military be the strongest and proudest of all armed forces around the world, and be looked at in the same light as they were, say twenty years ago! I can take any comments, questions or criticisms and would welcome the opportunity to speak with anyone who would like to discuss anything and everything in this book. The thing you and everyone needs to do is to try and get involved, do anything and everything in your power to make a difference. If everybody made a small difference a huge difference would result.

Just like in the first book some of the proceeds of this book will go to help injured soldiers and their families and also to care for animals all over the world. As I have said before, I cannot do it all, but I can do my part.